John Jacobson's
Silly Songs & Sing-Alongs

New Lyrics to Old Favorites

By John Jacobson

TABLE OF CONTENTS

HAL•LEONARD®
CORPORATION
7777 W. BLUEMOUND RD. P.O. BOX 13819 MILWAUKEE, WI 53213

As Happy as Can Be
(Tavern in the Town)

Arranged with New Lyrics by JOHN JACOBSON
Piano Accompaniment by DEAN CROCKER

Football!
(Hot Time in the Old Town)

Arranged with New Lyrics by JOHN JACOBSON
Piano Accompaniment by DEAN CROCKER

6

8

Must Be Autumn
(London Bridge)

Arranged with New Lyrics by JOHN JACOBSON
Piano Accompaniment by DEAN CROCKER

1st vs: Stretch arms slowly up as tall as you can

2nd vs: Slowly crouch down to a squatting position

3rd vs: Slowly stand and reach overhead

Corn is get - ting tall - er now, tall - er now, tall - er now.
Days are get - ting short - er now, short - er now, short - er now.
Corn is get - ting tall - er now, tall - er now, tall - er now.

2nd & 3rd vs: Slowly crouch to squat

All vs:
Lower "snow" hands like falling leaves

Corn is get - ting tall - er now. Must be Au - tumn!
Days are get - ting short - er now. Must be Au - tumn!
Days are get - ting short - er now. Must be

12

Für School Time
(Für Elise)

Arranged with New Lyrics by JOHN JACOBSON
Piano Accompaniment by DEAN CROCKER

Ev-'ry year I get to go to school, and as a
was a blast but now it's through, I bid a-

rule, I think it's cool. I see all my friend-ly teach-ers
dieu, to all I knew. E-ven though I'm los-ing my sun-

there, and though they glare, I know they care. Sum-mer
burn, as I re-turn I try to

SILLY SONGS & SING-ALONGS FOR FALL – Teacher Edition

Oh, Where Have You Been, Chris Columbus?
(Billy Boy)

Arranged with New Lyrics by JOHN JACOBSON
Piano Accompaniment by DEAN CROCKER

16

18

Goblins Don't Bother Me
(Shoo Fly)

Arranged with New Lyrics by JOHN JACOBSON
Piano Accompaniment by DEAN CROCKER

22

I Haven't Seen a Ghost All Day!
(Polly Wolly Doodle)

Arranged with New Lyrics by JOHN JACOBSON
Piano Accompaniment by DEAN CROCKER

When Skeletons Are Singing
(When Irish Eyes Are Smiling)

Arranged with New Lyrics by JOHN JACOBSON
Piano Accompaniment by DEAN CROCKER

30

There's a Nut in the Top of the Tree
(There's a Hole in the Bottom of the Sea)

Arranged with New Lyrics by JOHN JACOBSON
Piano Accompaniment by DEAN CROCKER

34

36

38

42

44

There's a Turkey in the Barnyard
(I've Been Working on the Railroad)

Arranged with New Lyrics by JOHN JACOBSON
Piano Accompaniment by DEAN CROCKER

This Is My Favorite Day
(Ta-Ra-Ra Boom-Dee-Ay)

Arranged with New Lyrics by JOHN JACOBSON
Piano Accompaniment by DEAN CROCKER

52

54

Santa, You Showed Up too Soon!
(My Bonnie Lies Over the Ocean)

Arranged with New Lyrics by JOHN JACOBSON
Piano Accompaniment by DEAN CROCKER

56

58

60

62

AS HAPPY AS CAN BE

(Tune: Tavern in the Town)
New Lyrics by John Jacobson

Come on!
We're gonna have some fun!
Have some fun!
Make way!
There's room for ev'ryone!
Ev'ryone!
Oh we will sing and play
And dance the Hootchie Coo!
So bring along a friend or two!

Come on do yourself a favor,
Bring along your friendly neighbor.
There will never be a better time
To do your best!

So, swing your partner to the left!
To the left!
Now swing your partner to the right!
To the right!
Why don't you clap your hands,
Come and sing along with me?
We're free and happy as can be!

(Dance break)
Though this song's a little sappy,
Ev'rybody here is happy.
This is not the time for anyone
To take a rest!

So swing your partner to the left!
To the left!
Now swing your partner to the right!
To the right!
Why don't you clap your hands,
Come and sing along with me?
We're free and happy as can be!
We're free and happy as can be!

FOOTBALL!

(Tune: Hot Time in the Old Town)
New Lyrics by John Jacobson

Football season is a shocking sight!
Ev'ry day and even Monday night!
Ninety games, if you have satellite!
The football season has fin'lly begun!
HOORAY!

Lots of folks who never play the game,
Love to give the referees the blame. *(You're blind!)*
Ev'ry weekend things are just the same.
The football season has fin'lly begun!
HOORAY!

(NFL Rap)
The teams of the AFC!
Bengals, Ravens, Titans, Browns,
Steelers, Chargers, Chiefs, Colts,
Texans, Broncos, Dolphins, Bills,
Patriots, Raiders, Jaguars, Jets.
The teams of the AFC!

This is just my favorite time of year,
When I wear my favorite football gear. *(Look out!)*
For my team I love to lead a cheer.
The football season has fin'lly begun!
HOORAY!

(NFL Rap)
The teams of the NFC!
Cardinals, Cowboys, Panthers, Bears,
Falcons, Lions, Giants, Niners,
Sea Hawks, Redskins, Packers, Saints,
Buccaneers, Vikings, Eagles, Rams.
The teams of the NFC!

Football season's really on a roll.
Family time is so out of control!
Can we make it past the Super Bowl?
The football season has finally,
I mean it! It's finally!
The season has fin'lly begun!
TOUCHDOWN!

MUST BE AUTUMN

(Tune: London Bridge)
New Lyrics by John Jacobson

Corn is getting taller now!
Taller now! Taller now!
Corn is getting taller now!
Must be Autumn!

Days are getting shorter now!
Shorter now! Shorter now!
Days are getting shorter now!
Must be Autumn!

Corn is getting taller now!
Taller now! Taller now!
Days are getting shorter now!
Must be Autumn!

The wind is really blowing now!
Blowing now! Blowing now!
The wind is really blowing now!
Must be Autumn!

The corn is getting taller now!
The days are getting shorter now!
The wind is really blowing now!
Must be Autumn!

All the leaves are falling down!
Falling down! Falling down!
All the leaves are falling down!
Must be Autumn!

Corn is getting taller now!
Shorter now! Blowing now!
All the leaves are falling down!
Must be Autumn!

FÜR SCHOOL TIME

(Tune: Für Elise)
New Lyrics by John Jacobson

Ev'ry year I get to go to school
And as a rule, I think it's cool.
I see all my friendly teachers there,
And though they glare, I know they care.

Summer was a blast but now it's through,
I bid adieu, to all I knew.
Even though I'm losing my sunburn,
As I return, I try to learn.

For ev'ry class, so much to know,
I'll never pass, but even so.
I'll try with all my might!

Then I will be glad I did my best,
With all the rest, I'll past the test!
I will always use the golden rule;
You see it's cool, to go to school!

For ev'ry class, so much to know,
I'll never pass, but even so.
I'll try with all my might!

Then I will be glad I did my best,
With all the rest, I'll past the test!
I will always use the golden rule;
You see it's cool, to go to school!

SILLY SONGS & SING-ALONGS FOR FALL – Teacher Edition

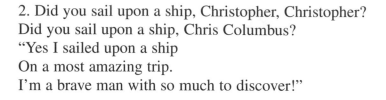

OH WHERE HAVE YOU BEEN, CHRIS COLUMBUS?

(Tune: Billy Boy)
New Lyrics by John Jacobson

1. Oh where have you been, Christopher, Christopher?
Oh where have you been, Chris Columbus?
"I have been across the sea!
And I think you will agree,
I'm a brave man with so much to discover!"

2. Did you sail upon a ship, Christopher, Christopher?
Did you sail upon a ship, Chris Columbus?
"Yes I sailed upon a ship
On a most amazing trip.
I'm a brave man with so much to discover!"

3. Did you find a brand new land, Christopher, Christopher?
Did you find a brand new land, Chris Columbus?
"Yes, I found a brand new land.
Stuck my flag there in the sand.
I'm a brave man with so much to discover!"

4. Was it fourteen ninety-two, Christopher, Christopher?
Was it fourteen ninety-two, Chris Columbus?
"It was fourteen ninety-two
That I sailed the ocean blue.
I'm a brave man with so much to discover!"

5. Did you find the world was round, Christopher, Christopher?
Did you find the world was round, Chris Columbus?
"Yes, I found the earth was round,
As I stood on solid ground.
I'm a brave man with so much to discover!"

6. Are you sure you were the first, Christopher, Christopher?
Are you sure you were the first, Chris Columbus?
"That's a bubble I must burst
For I wasn't quite the first,
But I'm a brave man with so much to discover."

Lyric Sheet

GOBLINS DON'T BOTHER ME

(Tune: Shoo Fly)
New Lyrics by John Jacobson

1. Goblins don't bother me.
Goblins don't bother me.
Goblins don't bother me,
For I'm as brave as I can be!
I am, I am, I am as brave as I can be.
I am, I am, I am as brave as a kid can be. Oh!

2. Witches don't bother me.
Witches don't bother me.
Witches don't bother me,
For I'm as brave as I can be.
I am, I am, I am as brave as I can be.
I am, I am, I am as brave as a kid can be. Oh!

3. Shadows don't bother me.
Shadows don't bother me.
Shadows don't bother me,
For I'm as brave as I can be.
I am, I am, I am as brave as I can be.
I am, I am, I am as brave as a kid can be. Oh!

4. Goblins don't bother me.
Witches don't bother me.
Shadows don't bother me,
For I'm as brave as I can be!
BOO!

I HAVEN'T SEEN A GHOST ALL DAY!

(Tune: Polly Wolly Doodle)
New Lyrics by John Jacobson

1. Oh I went outside to trick or treat,
But I haven't seen a ghost all day!
Lots of treats I like to eat,
But I haven't seen a ghost all day!
Halloween! Halloween!
My favorite day all year!
Though I thought I saw a goblin
And I heard two witches squabblin'
Still I haven't seen a ghost all day!

2. I thought I saw a kangaroo,
But I haven't seen a ghost all day!
A Frankenstein as big as you,
But I haven't seen a ghost all day!
Halloween! Halloween!
My favorite day all year!
Though I thought I saw a goblin
And I heard two witches squabblin'
Still I haven't seen a ghost all day!

3. I know I saw Count Dracula,
But I haven't seen a ghost all day!
A scarecrow with a head of straw,
But I haven't seen a ghost all day!
Halloween! Halloween!
My favorite day all year!
Though I thought I saw a goblin
And I heard two witches squabblin'
Still I haven't seen a ghost all day!

4. *Look! Up there behind that tree!*
Oh, I haven't seen a ghost all day!
Hurry up! Let's run away!
For I think I saw a ghost today!
Halloween! Halloween!
My favorite day all year!
Though I thought I saw a goblin
And I heard two witches squabblin'
And I think I saw a ghost today!
BOO!!

WHEN SKELETONS ARE SINGING

(Tune: When Irish Eyes Are Smiling)
New Lyrics by John Jacobson

1. When skeletons are singing,
You can hear them moan and groan.
And when skeletons are swinging,
It can chill you to the bone!
When skeletons are dancing,
If you want to do what's smart.
When you see their bones advancing,
You should get a running start!

2. When skeletons are grinning,
It is not a happy day.
Like I said in the beginning,
You had best be on your way.
When skeletons are walking,
Oh it won't be any fun.
It can send your knees a-knocking,
Get a grip! You better run!

3. When skeletons are staring,
You are on the warning track.
If you find yourself despairing,
You had better not look back.
When skeletons are jiving,
That will be a telling clue.
Halloween is soon arriving.
You have found a friendly crew!
BOO!

THERE'S A NUT IN THE TOP OF THE TREE

(Tune: There's a Hole in the Bottom of the Sea)
New Lyrics by John Jacobson

1. There's a NUT in the top of the tree.
(repeat)
There's a nut. There's a nut.
There's a NUT in the top of the tree.

2. There's a LEAF floating 'round
By the nut in the top of the tree.
(repeat)
There's a leaf. There's a leaf.
There's a LEAF floating 'round
By the NUT in the top of the tree.

3. There's a SQUIRREL looking up
At the LEAF floating 'round
By the NUT in the top of the tree.
(repeat)
There's a squirrel. There's a squirrel.
There's a SQUIRREL looking up
At the LEAF floating 'round
By the NUT in the top of the tree.

4. There's a TAIL on the SQUIRREL looking up
At the LEAF floating 'round
By the NUT in the top of the tree.
(repeat)
There's a tail. There's a tail.
There's a TAIL on the SQUIRREL looking up
At the LEAF floating 'round
By the NUT in the top of the tree.

5. There's a GOOSE flying south looking down
On the TAIL of the SQUIRREL looking up
At the LEAF floating 'round
By the NUT in the top of the tree.
(repeat)
There's a goose. There's a goose.
There's a GOOSE flying south looking down
On the TAIL of the SQUIRREL looking up
At the LEAF floating 'round
By the NUT in the top of the tree.

6. There's a FEATHER on the back
Of the GOOSE flying south looking down
On the TAIL of the SQUIRREL looking up
At the LEAF floating 'round
By the NUT in the top of the tree.
(repeat)
There's a feather. There's a feather.
There's a FEATHER on the back
Of the GOOSE flying south looking down
On the TAIL of the SQUIRREL looking up
At the LEAF floating 'round
By the NUT in the top of the tree.

7. There are SNOW FLAKES falling
On the FEATHER on the back
Of the GOOSE flying south looking down
On the TAIL of the SQUIRREL looking up
At the LEAF floating 'round
By the NUT in the top of the tree.
(repeat)
There are flakes, lots of flakes.
There are SNOW FLAKES falling
On the FEATHER on the back
Of the GOOSE flying south looking down
On the TAIL of the SQUIRREL looking up
At the LEAF floating 'round
By the NUT in the top of the tree.

8. There's a NUT getting cold
From the SNOW falling down
On the FEATHER on the back
Of the GOOSE flying south looking down
On the TAIL of the SQUIRREL looking up
At the LEAF floating 'round
By the NUT in the top of the tree.
(repeat)
There's a nut! We're all nuts!
There's a NUT getting cold
From the SNOW falling down
On the FEATHER on the back
Of the GOOSE flying south looking down
On the TAIL of the SQUIRREL looking up
At the LEAF floating 'round
By the NUT in the top of the tree!
WHEW!!

Lyric Sheet

THERE'S A TURKEY IN THE BARNYARD
(Tune: I've Been Working on the Railroad)
New Lyrics by John Jacobson

1. There's a turkey in the barnyard,
Big and proud and fat!
There's a turkey in the barnyard.
He's gobbling this and that.
How he likes to show his feathers
See his stately pace.
Puttin' two and two together,
He thinks he owns the place!

That turkey's gotta go!
That turkey's gotta go!
That puffed up piece of poultry's
Gotta go–oh-oh!
That turkey's gotta go!
That turkey's gotta go!
That puffed up piece of poultry's
Gotta go!

2. There's a turkey in the schoolyard,
Big and fat and proud.
There's a turkey in the schoolyard,
Where turkeys aren't allowed!
He can't even read a schoolbook.
He can't read or write,
But he thinks he has a cool look
And he gobbles day and night!

That turkey's gotta go!
That turkey's gotta go!
That puffed up piece of poultry's
Gotta go–oh-oh!
That turkey's gotta go!
That turkey's gotta go!
That puffed up piece of poultry's
Gotta go!

Fee fi, fiddlee–i-o!
Fee fi, fiddlee–i-o-o-o-o!
Fee fi fiddlee–i-o!
That puffed up piece of poultry's gotta go!

3. There's a turkey in the oven,
Lying upside down.
There's a turkey in the oven.
He's turning golden brown.
Gee! He's missing all his feathers,
Underneath the heat.
Looks a bit under the weather
But good enough to eat!

That turkey had to go!
That turkey had to go!
That puffed up piece of poultry
Had to go–oh-oh!
That turkey had to go!
That turkey had to go!
That puffed up piece of poultry
Had to go!

THIS IS MY FAVORITE DAY

(Tune: Ta-Ra-Ra Boom-Dee-Ay)
New Lyrics by John Jacobson

1. Each November we all meet.
All our relatives we greet.
Everybody takes a seat.
And we have a lot to eat!
Mashed potatoes piling high,
Mounds of muffins multiply,
Grandma makes a pumpkin pie;
Nothing here in short supply!

Oh what a bumper crop!
Can't see the tabletop!
The party never stops!
Let's eat until we pop!
Oh what a happy day!
Let's have a big buffet!
No matter what they say,
I love Thanksgiving Day!

2. Like a diamond in the rough,
Got a turkey we can stuff.
I can never get enough.
Overeating can be tough!
Plenty here for all of you.
All we do is chomp and chew.
Have a rutabaga too.
Every year we overdo!

Oh what a bumper crop!
Can't see the tabletop!
The party never stops!
Let's eat until we pop!
Oh what a happy day!
Let's have a big buffet!
Tomorrow we will pay!
I love Thanksgiving Day!

SANTA, YOU SHOWED UP TOO SOON!

(Tune: My Bonnie Lies Over the Ocean)
New Lyrics by John Jacobson

1. I went to the mall to go shopping.
Now what do you think I should see?
Although it is not close to winter,
They've put up a big Christmas tree!

2. Now taking his place at the center,
High on his velvety throne;
Beneath all the holly and ivy,
Saint Nicholas sits all alone!

Santa! Santa! Santa, you showed up
too soon, too soon!
Santa! Santa! Dear Santa,
you showed up too soon!

Jingle bells! Jingle bells!
Jingle all the way!   *(NOT YET!!)*

3. It seems that you're rushing the season.
We've only just fell into fall!
So Santa, please listen to reason.
You've shown up too soon at the Mall!

On the first day of Christmas
my true love gave to me.   *(STOP!!)*

4. Dear Santa, it's only October!
We really don't want to be mean.
Thanksgiving is not even over.
Can't we just enjoy Halloween?

Jolly Old Saint Nicholas
Lean your ear this way!   *(NO WAY!!)*

Santa! Santa! Dear Santa, you showed up
too soon, too soon!
Santa! Santa! Dear Santa, you showed up too …

Deck the hall with boughs of holly!
Fa la la la la la la la   *(NOT!!)*

5. Dear Santa, you showed up too early.
Dear Santa, you showed up too soon!
Yes Santa, you showed up too early!
We love you but we just passed June!

Up on the housetop reindeer pause,
Out jumps good old Santa Claus!
(ARGH! SEE WHAT I MEAN?)

6. Dear Santa, I'm writing this letter.
I hope that it gets through to you.
There's no one that I could like better,
But go home, you have work to do!

Santa! Santa! Oh Santa, you showed up
Too soon! Too soon!
Santa! Santa! Dear Santa, you showed up too …

Joy to the World!
Oh, Santa, you showed up …
We wish you a Merry Christmas!
Dear Santa, you showed up too soon!